THE MINSTREL BOY – THOMAS MOORE AND HIS MELODIES

to Mary Murphy

First published in 2001 by
Mercier Press
5 French Church St Cork
Tel: (021) 275040; Fax: (021) 274969; e.mail: books@mercier.ie
16 Hume Street Dublin 2
Tel: (01) 661 5299; Fax: (01) 661 8583; e.mail: books@marino.ie

Trade enquiries to CMD Distribution 55A Spruce Avenue
Stillorgan Industrial Park Blackrock County Dublin
Tel: (01) 294 2556; Fax: (01) 294 2564
e.mail: cmd@columba.ie

© Sean McMahon 2001
A CIP record for this book is available from the British Library.

ISBN 1 85635 350 8
10 9 8 7 6 5 4 3 2 1

Cover design by Penhouse Design
Printed in Ireland by ColourBooks Baldoyle Dublin 13

THE MINSTREL BOY –
THOMAS MOORE
AND HIS MELODIES

SEAN McMAHON

MERCIER PRESS

2648187 , 920
ΠOO

CONTENTS

Chronology   7

1 'The Young May Moon'   9

2 'And Folly's All They've Taught Me'   20

3 'Let Erin Remember . . . '   30

4 'Go Where Glory Waits Thee'   40

5 'When in Death I Shall Calm Recline'   47

A Selection of Moore's Verse   53

Select Bibliography   80

CHRONOLOGY

1779	Born at 12 Aungier Street on 28 May, first-born of John Moore, a grocer from Kerry, and Anastasia Codd, daughter of a Wexford merchant
1793	Hobart's Catholic Relief Act, removing many Catholic disabilities and permitting them to enter Trinity College Dublin, passed
1794	Moore enrolled as an undergraduate in Trinity
1798	Visitation of Trinity by Fitzgibbon and Duigenan; Moore's interrogation under oath; United Irishmen's rising
1799	Moore enrolled in Middle Temple, London, to study law
1800	*Odes of Anacreon* published by John Stockdale, London
1801	*Poetical Works of 'Thomas Little'* published by J. & T. Carpenter, London
1803	Appointed Admiralty Registrar of Bermuda; Robert Emmet executed
1804	Tours East Coast states of America and visits Canada
1806	*Epistles, Odes and Other Poems* published by Carpenter; Moore almost fights duel with Francis Jeffrey
1808	First and second numbers of *Irish Melodies* published by Power Brothers
1811	Marries Bessy Dyke of Kilkenny; becomes friendly with Lord Byron, despite having challenged him to a duel

1812	Birth of daughter Barbara
1813	Birth of daughter Anastatia
1814	Birth of daughter Olivia
1815	Death of Olivia
1817	*Lalla Rookh: An Oriental Romance* published by Longmans; defalcation by Moore's Bermuda deputy leaves Moore liable for his debts of £6,000
1818	Birth of son Thomas
1819–22	Exile in Paris and Italy; meets Byron and is given the poet's *Memoirs*
1823	Birth of son Russell
1826	Death of daughter Barbara
1829	Death of daughter Anastatia
1830	*The Life of Lord Byron*, published by John Murray
1831	*The Life and Death of Lord Edward Fitzgerald* published by Longmans
1835	Triumphal visit to Ireland
1842	Death of son Russell
1845	Death of son Thomas
1849	Onset of senility
1852	Dies at Sloperton on 26 February and is buried in Bromham Churchyard
1865	Bessy Moore dies in October and is buried beside her husband and children

1

'THE YOUNG MAY MOON'

The first child and only son of John Moore, grocer and wine merchant, who hailed from Kerry, and Anastatia Codd, the eldest daughter of a Wexford provision merchant, was born above his father's shop at 12 Aungier Street, Dublin, on 28 May 1779. The family were comfortably off by the standards of the time and were beginning to enjoy the alleviation of the Popery Laws, which had effectively rendered Irish Catholics non-citizens. The penal enactments were ingenious but flawed in their purpose of maintaining an exclusive Protestant Ascendancy: the learned professions – except, surprisingly, that of medicine – were barred to Catholics; they could not own land and they had no political existence. There was, however, nothing to prevent a restless entrepreneurial instinct making the lucky and the industrious very rich, especially in the cities, and as soon as the limited amelioration (granted mainly out of political necessity) became effective, a kind of commercial Catholic ascendancy were allowed to educate their children at home.

By the time of young Tom's birth, there was little, if any, prevention of Catholic worship, and a Catholic hierarchy, more loyal to the British Crown than any Protestant, had begun to build up the Church into the dominant feature of Irish political and social life that it was to remain for another two centuries. He 'was baptised according to the rite of the Catholic Church on the 30th day of May AD 1779', as the certificate kept by him records. His mother was not yet twenty and, though considerably younger than her husband, became the dynamo of the family. She used to chide the easygoing father: 'You know, Jack, you were an old bachelor when I married you.' With confident foresight, she had the insignia erased from a gold crown-piece and inscribed with the name and birth date of the wunderkind. It was to be the first of many similar decorations.

It was soon clear that this child was gifted with great intelligence, a fine sense of dramatic utterance, a true and sweet singing voice and a charm that made all the women in his life his willing slaves. Even more remarkably, he was just as popular with his schoolfellows. He managed to be bright at his lessons without becoming detested, a considerable achievement in itself, and continued to be liked throughout his life by most of the people he met. He was blessed with a sunny disposition, a boyish innocence and delight in company, and he was aware of his remarkable facility in the fashioning of elegant verse. Like Pope, another child prodigy, he 'lisped in numbers for the numbers came.' He published his first book, a translation from the Greek of the *Odes* Anacreon (born c. 570 BC) in 1800 and *The Poetical Works of the Late Thomas Little Esq.* when he was just twenty-two.

The 'RG' who wrote his entry in the Dictionary of National Biography refers with Victorian disapproval to Moore's 'original amorous poetry, exceptionable on the grounds of morality, and with no conspicuous literary recommendation except its sprightliness'. Even Byron, later one of his closest friends, chides him tongue-in-cheek in *English Bards and Scotch Reviewers* (1809):

> Who in soft guise surrounded by a choir
> Of virgins melting, not to Vesta's fire,
> With sparkling eyes and cheek by passion
>   flush'd
> Strikes his wild lyre, whilst listening
>   dames are hush'd?
> 'Tis Little! young Catullus of his day,
> As sweet, but as immoral, in his lay.

In reality, lines like:

> 'Cease, cease!' the blushing girl replied,
> And in her milky arms she caught me –
> 'How can you thus your pupil chide?
> You know 'twas in the dark you taught me!'

were no more likely to shock Regency society than that of the present day.

The ability to translate from the original Greek and to devise modern equivalents suggests a talent more than sprightly. Young Tom was usually top of his class in the grading system of the day but he worked hard and his ambitious mother saw to it that he maintained that position. When still a pre-teen, he was put over his lessons by Anastatia, who several times woke her boy at two in the morning when she returned home from an active, if decorous, social life to hear his book. At a kind of public prize-giving she railed at the teacher when bigger boys tried to oust Tom from the 'dux' position. (It was not hard to be bigger than her bijou son, who never grew beyond five feet.)

His excellence in the ancient classics was due not so much to the famous Samuel Whyte – whose academy he attended and to whom he dedicated a much appreciated ode – as to 'Old Donovan', Whyte's usher, who not only ground the young scholar in Latin and Greek but completed his patriotic education. By the time Moore was ready for entrance to Trinity, looking absurdly young, he knew his Irish history and legendary lore as well as the glories of the ancient classics. His parents were strongly nationalist in their outlook but, like many Catholics in their position, could not risk overt opposition to the government. One of the paradoxes of the career of their gifted son was that, although he was the darling of Whig drawing rooms, he never compromised in his patriotism and he earned for his people the same kind of confused respect among the English as his friend Sir Walter Scott had won for his over-the-border countrymen.

One of the terms of Robert Hobart's Catholic Relief Act of 1793 was that Catholics be allowed to take degrees at Trinity, but, with typical meanness, they were not made eligible for scholarships. This was the obvious next step for the son of whom the Moores had such expect-ations. He was registered as a member of the university in June 1794 just after his fifteenth birthday and began attendance in January of the following year. He had already begun his trans-lation of the Anacreon odes, having been granted access to the remarkable library founded in 1701 by Archbishop Narcissus Marsh (1638–1713) in St Patrick's Cathedral Close. It was intended by the founder that the subscribers should be 'all graduates and gentlemen' and it must have pleased the undergraduate to realise which category he logically fell into.

Life at Trinity was a disappointment to the talented and ambitious Moore, especially since he was better equipped in Classics than many of the fellows. He had of course the *aoibhinn beatha an scoláire* and enjoyed it hugely. Trinity could not help reflecting, at least among its students, the spirit of the times, and it was known that one of Moore's friends, Robert Emmet (1778-1803), was, like his brother Thomas, a member of the United Irishmen, a revolutionary society that had been founded in 1791 in Belfast by, among others, a Trinity graduate, Wolfe Tone (1763–98). Though they were close friends, Emmet, with exquisite tact, never tried to interest his friend in his radical activities, sensing, as Moore afterwards admitted, that he was 'constantly tied to his mother's apron strings'. On one occasion Moore did strut a bit and wrote an anonymous pamphlet, signed 'A Patriotic Freshman', that ended with the stirring words: 'We should all Unite, rally round her [Ireland's] standard and recover our Heaven-born rights, our principles from the grasp of Tyranick masters.' Emmet advised him courteously but firmly that he preferred that no attention should be focused upon politics in the college.

It was clear, however, that Emmet was already dedicated to revolution. As Moore recorded in his *Memoirs* (a document full of the spirit of the truth if not always precise in detail), he was once playing the tune to which he afterwards wrote the words of 'Let Erin Remember' when Emmet cried, 'Oh that I were at the head of 20,000 men marching to that air!' It was a period of effective government infiltration with a successful system of police spies and it was not long before the lord chancellor, John Fitzgibbon, Earl of Clare (1749–1802), and the advocate-general, 'Paddy' Duigenan, visited the college to examine the students individually as to their loyalty. Emmet refused to attend for the inquisition and was deemed to have left the university, but the unheroic Moore was in a quandary – as were his parents. It was his first ordeal, a clash between honour and expediency – and he solved it in a typically Tommyish way, as he recalls in his *Memoirs*:

At the Tribunal sat the formidable Fitz-gibbon, whose name I never heard con-nected but with domineering insolence and cruelty; and by his side the memorable 'Paddy' Duigenan – memorable at least to all who lived in those dark times for his eternal pamphlets sounding the tocsin against the Catholics.

He approached the table and announced that he had an objection to taking the oath. Fitzgibbon looked down at this cherub, who looked more like twelve years of age than just short of eighteen, and said sternly that he could not remain at the college if he did not take the oath. 'I shall then take the oath, still reserving the right of refusing such questions as I have described,' Moore replied. (He had said a few moments before that he did not fear to incriminate himself but would not accuse others.) The questioning was uncharacteristically short and easy, and Moore was allowed to stand down. Before he left, Fitzgibbon, prompted by the relentless Duigenan, asked: 'When such are the answers you are able to give, pray what was the cause of your great repugnance to taking the oath?' Tommy, with a look of great sincerity, answered, 'It was the first oath I ever took and it was, I think, a very natural hesitation.' One of the fellows was heard to say, 'That's the best answer that has been given yet!' The combination of puckish looks and instinctive acting ability had won again.

Many years later, when the Minstrel Boy was at the height of his fame, the begrudgers of the 'blind and ignorant town', as Yeats described their birthplace, were fond of quoting Byron's comment, 'Tommy loves a lord!' The truth was that, for all his active life, many lords loved Tommy. He was – perhaps judiciously – ill when the '98 rebellion took place, but he recollected how dramatic the effect of the lights going out all over Dublin had been that May night. On 25 September 1803 he embarked to take up the post of registrar of the naval prize-court in Bermuda, a sinecure obtained for him by his patron and friend, Francis Rawdon-Hastings, Lord Moira (1754–1826). Five days earlier, his college friend had been brutally executed in Thomas Street. Emmet's speech from the dock had asked from the world 'the charity of its silence'. Moore made no comment about the friend of his youth at the time of the execution, but in 1808, in the first number of the *Irish Melodies* he included his most obvious verse tribute to Emmet in 'Oh, Breathe Not His Name'. Emmet was also the inspiration for 'The Minstrel Boy' and 'Lay His Sword by His Side'. It was Moore, too, who made Emmet's fiancée, Sarah Curran (d. 1808) eternally famous as the subject of 'She Is Far from the Land' (1811).

Moore never forgot his friend; there are twenty references to him in the *Memoirs, Journals and Correspondence*, which were published in eight volumes between 1853 and 1858. (These were edited by Moore's friend Lord John Russell (1792–1878), who was twice prime minister.) In one, the unrepentant nationalist was pleased to record: 'Well, thank God, I have lived to pronounce a eulogium upon Robert Emmett [sic] at the Irish Chief Secretary's table.'

2

'AND FOLLY'S ALL
THEY'VE TAUGHT ME'

Moore graduated BA in 1798 and in March 1799, Dick Whittington-like, went off to London to seek his fortune – or rather, to enrol in the Middle Temple to became a lawyer like his greater precursor, Daniel O'Connell. The account of his leaving of Inishfallen in the *Memoirs* nicely combines a mock-heroic epical air with mundane details that make it, even at this distance, rather touching:

A part of the small sum which I took with me was in guineas, and I recollect was carefully sewn up by my mother into the waistband of my pantaloons. There was also another treasure, which she had, unknown to me, sewed up in some other part of my clothes; that was a scapular (as it was called), a small bit of cloth, blessed by a priest, which a fond superstition inclined her to believe would keep the wearer of it from harm. And thus, with this charm about me, of which I was wholly unconscious, and my little packet of guineas, of which I felt deeply the responsibility, did I for the first time start from home for the great world of London.

Life was austere enough at the beginning but the next few years were to make it clear that the young man's career would not lie in the courts. He was very homesick at first and his letters to his mother (written twice a month while she lived) are full of the anticipation of seeing Dublin again. He had learned that 'the Parkgate way is not by the half so much. So *that* shall be the way by which I shall return, for I will certainly, by God's will, see you in the summer.' (The journey over by Holyhead had been long and stormy, and Parkgate, then a busy port on the Dee in Cheshire, was Liverpool's predecessor until silting up robbed it of its career as a packet station.) Yet by the August of the next year he was able to write, in justifiable self-congratulation:

> I was yesterday introduced to his Royal
> Highness, George, Prince of Wales. He is
> beyond doubt a man of fascinating manners.
> When I was presented to him, he said he
> was very happy to know *a man of my
> abilities;* and when I thanked him for the
> honour he did me in permitting the dedi-
> cation of *Anacreon* he stopped me and said
> the honour was *entirely* his in being *allowed*
> to put his name to a work of such merit . . .
> Is not all this very fine? But, my dearest
> mother, it has cost me a *new coat . . .*

When he wished, he could be a master of bathos.

The change in his fortunes – and career – was largely due to Lord Moira, who as a favour to Moore's good friend of the Ordnance Board in Dublin, Joe Atkinson, asked the young man to call upon him. Moira, unusually for an English officer, had had a distinguished career in the American war and was a strong Catholic

Emancipationist. He had a house on the south quays in Dublin and a large estate at Donington Park in Derbyshire, and was a sterling patron of the arts. He became the young man's patron and introduced him into the great Liberal houses of England. He and Atkinson devised a scheme to make him a kind of Irish Poet Laureate, but Moore refused. In this matter his usually reticent father gave him sound advice, writing and urging him to refuse, while reassuring him that his mother and sisters, Catherine and Ellen, were not 'in instant necessity'. Moore himself could be quite adamant about receiving favours and, though this one would have provided him with a steady, if small, income, he was afraid that it would make him the government's creature. (The English laureate at the time was Henry James Pye, of whom little has been heard since.) Instead, he accepted Moira's invitation to stay at Donington for as long and as often as he liked; a apartment was prepared for him and he had the use of his lordship's extensive library.

The opening of so many doors increased the number of possible subscribers for his books. When trying to find a subscription list for *Anacreon*,

Moore was uncharacteristically sharp about the fellows of his Alma Mater, complaining that, apart from the Provost and his tutor, 'not one of the scoundrelly monks of Trinity has subscribed to the work'. It was published in July 1800 and the grocer's son became known throughout fashionable society as 'Anacreon' Moore, the witty, deliciously naughty little Irishman who could literally sing for his supper. This slightly racy reputation was confirmed with the publication of *The Poetical Works of 'Thomas Little'* in 1801. Indeed it was only with the coming of the first series of the more decorous *Irish Melodies* in 1808 that Moore lost his reputation for fashionable licentiousness. In a way the reputation was his own fault. Some of the 'Little' poems were versions of the lyrics of the Roman poet Catullus (c. 84–c. 54 BC), whose work was regarded as ripe even in the latter days of the Republic.

The beginning of the new century saw the start of a gradual change in public taste. With the growth of a respectable bourgeoisie and a reading public that was not aristocratic, the bald locutions of the eighteenth century were becoming offensive. The new queen would not be

crowned for another thirty-seven years but
Victorian morality was already slouching towards
Balmoral to be born.

Poems such as 'The Catalogue' and lines like:

> Pity, then poor Jessy's ruin,
> Who becalm'd by Slumber's wing,
> Never felt what love was doing –
> Never dream'd of such a thing!'

suggested that the poet knew whereof he spake.
A poem written at the end of his American tour
to the wife of the consul at Norfolk, Virginia,
seemed to suggest that the 'young Catullus' was
still active:

> But oh! 'twould ruin saints to see
> Those tresses thus unbound and free,
> Adown your shoulders sweeping;
> They put such thoughts into one's head
> Of deshabillé, and night and bed,
> And – anything but sleeping!

It was inevitable that 'Anacreon' Moore and all
his works and pomps should fall foul of the

rugged and puritanical pen of Francis, later Lord, Jeffrey (1773–1850) of the *Edinburgh Review*. Jeffrey's notice on 'Thomas Little' was devastating: phrases like 'stimulating his jaded fancy for new images of impurity' and 'gently perverting the most simple and generous of their affections' were damning enough, but when Moore was accused of wholesale corruption and charged that the book's 'reputation and its influence will descend with the greater effect to the great body of the community' it was too much. He felt obliged to challenge Jeffrey to a duel. (The soaring sales which followed Jeffrey's review, incidentally, brought little reward to the author; he had made the first of many bad deals with a publisher.)

Resort to 'satisfaction', though illegal, was not uncommon at the time, but it was discovered by the seconds as the parties assembled on the morning of 15 August 1806 at Chalk Farm that neither gentleman had ever handled a pistol before. Horner, Jeffrey's second, did not even know how to load, and relied upon Hume, Moore's man, to prepare both pistols. In the delay that followed, the principals began to chat and were sorry to have to get down to business. Just as they were taking aim, a party of police officers arrived and carted the duellists off to Bow Street. There, in the same cell, they discussed Ireland, Scotland and literature – and became friends for life.

The duel won Moore another friend, in a typically oblique Mooreish manner. Lord Byron (1788–1824), who had been delighted with the 'Little' poems when he was an adolescent, was himself savaged in the *Edinburgh* in January 1808. His juvenile collection *Hours of Idleness* was shredded by Lord Brougham (1778–1868) and he responded with the splendid Popean satire *English Bards and Scottish Reviewers* the following year. The book was a brilliant piece of work for a twenty-year-old and included this attack on the editor of the *Edinburgh:*

Health to great Jeffrey! Heaven preserve
    his life,
To flourish on the fertile shores of Fife,
And guard it sacred in its future wars,
Since authors sometimes seek the field of
    Mars!
Can none remember that eventful day,

That ever-glorious, almost fatal fray,
When Little's leadless pistol met his eye
And Bow-street myrmidons stood
    laughing by?

There had, as we have seen, been difficulties with the loading of the pistols and, when the magistrate examined them, at least one was empty. The humiliating suggestion that the duel had been staged was too much, however. To use a line that brought the house down when Moore spoke it in *A Castle in Andalusia,* a play by John O'Keefe (1747–1833), at a festival in Kilkenny: 'True anger raises me; I always appear six foot in a passion.' He wrote a strong note to the notorious lord but Byron was out of the country when it was delivered. And when the two actually met, mutual admiration led to a lasting friendship. Byron dedicated *The Corsair* (1814) to Moore and made him the custodian of his memoirs; Moore wrote Byron's life story in 1830, six years after the death of the meteor. It is hard to believe now that, in his day, the Irish poet's work was much more highly regarded than that of the mad, bad earl. One of Byron's deservedly less well-known *Occasional Pieces* (to be sung to the tune of 'Eileen Aroon') begins:

> What are you doing now?
> Oh Thomas Moore?
> What are you doing now?
> Oh Thomas Moore?
> Sighing or suing now,
> Rhyming or wooing now,
> Billing or cooing,
> Which, Thomas Moore?

In fact, when the tribute was written, the billing and cooing had become licit; Thomas Little, the charming, voluble rake, had become the respectable married Mr Moore, with a beautiful little wife, sixteen years his junior. When Byron left in 1817 to fulfil his destiny at Missolonghi, he wrote a five-stanza farewell to the well-known author of the *Irish Melodies*, simple but sincere:

> My boat is on the shore,
> And my bark is on the sea;
> But before I go, Tom Moore,
> Here's a double health to thee!

3

'LET ERIN REMEMBER . . . '

Moore had generous patronage from a number of Whig aristocrats and, while he remained a bachelor, could depend for both shelter and sustenance on lordly invitations. When he married, his entrée into fashionable drawing rooms might have diminished, but his wife was on the whole content to live at a tactful distance from the Season. Bessie Dyke (?1794–1865) was of lowly origin by the social standards of the time. Her father was a dancing master and when Moore met her in Kilkenny in 1809 she was a professional actress. The annual theatre festival was the highlight of the self-conscious town's artistic and social life. Moore, who had been an accomplished actor since his schooldays – some detractors said he acted all the time – was one of the stars, and it was, appropriately, as the eponymous 'Peeping Tom' that he played opposite the most beautiful member of the Dyke family as Lady Godiva in a play that was *not* one of the Coventry cycle.

They were married on 25 March 1811 in St Martin's Church in London and spent their long honeymoon in Donington Park, later moving to a cottage in nearby Kegworth in Leicestershire. There, as Moore wrote in a letter to his friend Lady Donegall (d. 1828) in May 1812, 'she runs wild about a large garden.' Financially as well as socially, the marriage seemed ill-advised, yet it turned out to be the most sensible move the often reckless Moore ever made. They were happy in each other for as long as he lived, though their lives were to be blighted by early senility in the husband and the deep sadness of the premature deaths of their children, Barbara (1812–26), Anastasia (1813–29), Olivia Byron (1814–15), Tom (1818–45) and John Russell (1823–42).

Moore was generous, perhaps a little spend-thrift, and his dealings with publishers, with the honourable exception of Longmans, were not usually to his advantage. His slightly cavalier attitude to matters fiscal and financial on one occasion caused him serious trouble. The Bermuda sinecure obtained by Moira had enabled him to broaden his horizons and had given him a chance of travel and amorous adventures in the United States and Canada in 1804. As was the practice, he appointed a deputy (called Sheddon) to carry out his duties at the Bermudan naval court. In 1817, when he 'seemed at the summit of fame and fortune', as the Dictionary of National Biography dramatically put it, he heard that Sheddon had defaulted with £5,000 – a huge sum of money in those years. Offers of loans came from all sides, including one of £1,000 from Jeffrey, but, proud as always, Moore rejected them.

It was necessary, however, that he should take himself out of the jurisdiction until the matter could be settled. He went to Paris in 1819 and, joined by his friend Lord John Russell, did a kind of Grand Tour that included a visit to Italy, meeting Byron in Venice and taking the poet's *Memoirs* into his safe keeping. The debt was reduced to £1,000, which was paid by his friend Lord Landsdowne (1780–1862), and

Moore was able to return home to England in 1822. It was typical of him that he immediately secured a draft from Longmans for the amount, using the Byron *Memoirs* as collateral.

Whatever about the much-appreciated patronage that undoubtedly helped Moore gain subscribers for his publications, he regarded himself, with justice, as a working writer. The bibliography of his publications lists sixty-seven different items. He was primarily a poet, who wrote verse-romances, satires and exquisite song lyrics. He was also a biographer, writing early lives of Richard Brinsley Sheridan (1825), Byron (1830) and the United Irishman Lord Edward Fitzgerald (1831). He published a *History of Ireland* (1835, 1837, 1840 and 1846) in four volumes, collaborated with Mozart's friend Michael Kelly on a musical play, *The Gipsy Prince* (1801), and ten years later devised a comic opera, *M.P., or The Blue Stocking*.

Yet his lasting fame rests with his 'Melodies' and 'Airs'. He was very aware of this himself and, to use a crude modernism, was an excellent 'plugger' of his own material. He made a lot of money with *Lalla Rookh* (1817), a highly scented oriental romance that is now largely unreadable. Its main claim to modern fame lies in its providing the opportunity for excellent parody. Lalla Rookh, the daughter of the Muslim tyrant Al Hassan, who 'loves – but knows not whom she loves /Nor what his race nor whence he came' complains:

> I never nursed a dear gazelle
> To glad me with its soft black eye,
> But when it came to love me well
> And love me, it was sure to die!

(In this, the gazelles cleverly anticipated their mistress's inevitable fate.) This was crying out for parody; the most famous (and printable) one was by James Payn (1830–98):

> I never had a piece of toast
> Particularly long and wide,
> But fell upon the sanded floor,
> *And* always *on the buttered side.*

Writing to his publisher Thomas Longman in 1827, Moore commented: 'With what you say about *Lalla Rookh* being the "cream of the copyrights", perhaps it may in a *property* sense; but I am strongly inclined to think that, in a race into future times (if *anything* of mine could pretend to such a run), those little ponies, the "Melodies", will beat the mare, Lalla Rookh, hollow.' The *Melodies* might have been a creamy copyright too if Moore had had a publisher for them as honourable as Tom Longman. As it was, the Powers brothers paid him a dole of £500 a year, for long his only source of income, to write and sing Irish melodies, while they made a fortune on them.

His reputation outside his own censorious city and country has remained high, but a kind of ambivalence about him persisted in post-revolutionary Ireland. After nearly a century of concert and popular fame, his Irish songs began to embarrass not only the Gaelic purists, who felt that the grafting of, at times, inappropriate lyrics to traditional Irish airs was some kind of betrayal, but even the ordinary folk, who had learned 'Let Erin Remember' and 'The Minstrel Boy' at school and had a passing acquaintance with at least a score of others. Criticism had begun early: Edward Bunting (1773–1843), who had noted down some of the airs at the Belfast Harp Festival of 1792 and published them in 1796 and 1806, claimed that they had been distorted to fit Moore's lyrics by Sir John Stevenson (c. 1760–1833), who made the arrangements and introduced them with operatic flourish.

It was partly this floridity that caused the radical essayist William Hazlitt (1778–1830) to assail them in *The Spirit of the Age* (1825):

If these national airs do indeed express the soul of impassioned feeling in his countrymen, the cause of Ireland is hopeless. If these prettinesses pass for patriotism, if a country can tear from its heart's core only these vapid, varnished sentiments, lip-deep, and let its tears evaporate in an empty conceit, let it be governed as it has been. There are here no tones to waken Liberty, to console Humanity. Mr Moore converts the wild harp of Erin into a musical snuff-box.

Hazlitt was not the first (or last) Englishman to get Irish motives wrong. He (who had rather illogically hoped that Napoleon would conquer England and bring Liberty) required material as fiery as the stuff he wrote himself. Moore was not writing tunes to waken this Liberty but to indicate to the English that Ireland existed, and that she had a history and a culture in spite of two centuries of English occlusion. A much more sensible and practical judgement was that of Thomas Davis (1814–45). Davis realised that Moore had been a precursor in the work that he and Gavan Duffy were doing in the *Nation* . In one of his essays for that paper, he wrote: 'A reprint of Moore's *Melodies* on lower keys, and at much lower prices, would restore the sentimental music of Ireland to its natural supremacy.'

Another worshipper of 'Tommy' Moore was James Joyce, who as a tenor sang many of the Melodies and did not need Davis's recommended transposition. He was anxious, too, to teach them to young Georgio. In *Ulysses* Joyce's Everyman, Leopold Bloom, could not help noticing 'Tommy Moore's roguish finger' on the libellous statue at the junction of Westmoreland

and College Streets, and the fact that, placed beside a large urinal, it celebrates the meeting of the waters. Among English writers, Tennyson, Landor and Shelley were fans, and Charles Dickens has more than twenty-five references to the *Melodies* in his novels and stories: Inspector Bucket sings 'Believe Me' in *Bleak House* and it is also mentioned in *The Old Curiosity Shop*. Perhaps the greatest tribute to the *Melodies* was that of the German composer Friedrich Von Flotow (1812–83), who in 1847 lifted 'The Last Rose of Summer' bodily and transplanted it in his opera *Martha*.

Only one other of Moore's songs has parity with the 'little ponies'; 'Oft in the Stilly Night' was published in the first series of *National Airs* (1815) to a Russian melody and is thought by many to be his best work, though there are many others clamouring for that prize. If the present generation of Irish children has grown up without a knowledge of the harp that once through Tara's halls its soul of music shed, has not gone to the wars with the minstrel boy, has not seen with the fisherman on Lough Neagh's banks 'the round towers of other days in the waves beneath them shining' or parodied 'She Is Far from the Land', it is the first for 150 years. And is it not bereft? For whatever the purist and vocal patriots may have said about Moore, accusing him of failing in something he never attempted, he left behind a body of work which gave the downtrodden Irish a sentimental but real sense of identity. It not only succoured them at home but provided them with a transportable solace when, in their millions, they left. And only the most pachydermal can resist even now the songs, with their remarkable marriage of lyrics and music, which was the lyricist's sole intention. The 'little ponies', as he foretold, are with us still.

4

'GO WHERE GLORY WAITS THEE'

There were to be no more adventures for Moore after his return from France. In 1817 the family had moved to a cottage at Sloperton, near Devizes in Wiltshire, to be near the new patron, Lord Landsdowne. (Lord Moira had been made governor-general of India in 1813 and had, unaccountably, not taken Moore with him as his secretary.) It was to be their last move. After his Continental exile, they settled again in their spacious cottage, while Moore continued to bask in the glory of his contemporary fame and to be eternally strapped for money. His situation of having to continue to support his family by his pen, often by near hack work, was to be alleviated in 1835 by a literary pension of £300 a year, obtained for him by his friend Lord John Russell, and this was supplemented by £100 from the civil list in 1850. By this time, senile dementia had taken its grip. Further volumes of the *Irish Melodies* were published in 1821 and 1824, *Sacred Songs* in 1824 and collections of *National Airs* in 1822, 1826 and 1827.

Byron died in 1824 and his body was brought back to England to receive a fitting funeral for the hero of Greek resistance. The *Memoirs* that had been entrusted to Moore by the poet now involved him in some controversy that has redounded since – and not to his credit. He had sold them to John Murray, Byron's publisher, for 2,000 guineas in November 1821, on the understanding that they should not be published during Byron's lifetime. The Byron family appealed to Moore to recover them, Byron's widow even offering to pay him. The offer was characteristically refused; Moore found the money and the documents were destroyed – burned in front of witnesses. To modern eyes, such an act borders on sacrilege, but attitudes were different then; the family were anxious that the world should not discover just how – in Lady Caroline Lamb's words – mad, bad and dangerous to know Byron would seem.

Moore agonised over the deed but not for long; to use a phrase recorded in his journal at the time of young Tom's death: 'I thank God for my cheerful disposition.' The affair of the *Memoirs* was protracted and there were some who criticised Moore for accepting a commission from Murray to write Byron's biography, though strongly urged to do so by John Cam Hobhouse (1786–1869), the poet's closest friend. It was he who had insisted upon the destruction of the original text. As it turned out, the *Life of Lord Byron* (1830) was extremely successful, quickly paying for Murray's advance of £2,000 and netting both publisher and author a decent profit. As the custodian of the lost *Memoirs* for five years, Moore was in the best possible position to write the biography and for many decades it was the standard work on its subject – not uncritical but entirely empathetic.

Moore made a penultimate visit to Ireland in August 1835, when he was fifty-six. He travelled to Liverpool by the new railway and, to add great zest to his journey, learned at the port that Landsdowne had obtained the £300 pension for him. Crossing to Dublin, he stayed with his sister Ellen in North Cumberland Street and made a sentimental visit to Aungier Street. The proprietor, discovering who his grand visitor was, introduced him to his wife, crying, 'Here's Sir Thomas Moore, who was born in this house, come to ask us to let him see the rooms; and it's proud I am to have him under the old roof.' Next day there was a grand dinner at Trinity and a visit to the theatre, where the groundlings called: 'Don't be shy, Tom! Come show your Irish face!' The day ended with supper at the Viceregal Lodge.

He drove south by landau through the Vale of Avoca and the meeting of the waters which he had made famous, and on to Wexford town, where his grandfather Codd had kept his shop in the Cornmarket. (His mother had died in 1832, having survived her much older husband by seven years. Moore was not a man given to public mourning; he hated funerals and was reluctant to attend the obsequies of even his friend Byron. It was with great relief that he followed the advice of his mother and sister at his father's wake not to look at the corpse.) Death was, however, the furthest thing from his mind as he proceeded triumphally to Bannow, the bay where the invading Normans had built their first settlement:

When we arrived at the first triumphal arch, there was a decorated car and my Nine Muses, some of them remarkably pretty girls, particularly the one who placed the crown upon my head: and after we had proceeded a little way, seeing how much they were pressed by the crowd, I made her and two of her companions get up on the car behind me . . . As we proceeded slowly along, I said to my pretty muse behind me, 'This is a long journey for you!' 'O sir,' she replied, with a sweetness and kindness of look not to be found in more artificial life, 'I wish it was more than 300 miles.' It is curious and perhaps not to accounted for that, as I passed along in all this triumph, with so many cordial and sweet faces turned towards me, a feeling of deep sadness came more than once over my heart. Whether it might not have

been some of the Irish airs they played
that called up mournful associations
connected with the reverse of all that
smiling picture I know not, but it was so.

Truly, *'Erin! The tear and the smile in thine eyes /
Blend like the rainbow that hangs in thy skies.'* It was
at moments like these that he embodied the truth
stated so well in the introduction to the *Melodies:*

The tone of defiance, succeeded by the
languor of despondency – a burst of
turbulence dying away into softness – the
sorrows of one moment lost in the levity
of the next – and all that romantic mixture
of mirth and sadness, which is naturally
produced by the efforts of a lively tem-
perament to shake off or forget the wrongs
that lie upon it. Such are the features of
our history and character, which we find
strongly and faithfully reflected in our
music . . .

Moore's patriotism, indeed nationalism, was never
in doubt; at a time when tact might have won him

real political advancement, he wrote in the *Life
and Death of Lord Edward Fitzgerald* (1831) an
account of the career of a revolutionary, however
aristocratic, who wished to throw off the yoke of
England. This rashness placed him in danger of
losing the patronage of his own loving lords. He
went further, claiming in the book that, among all
the men he had ever known who combined 'pure
moral worth with intellectual power, I should,
among the highest of the few, place Robert
Emmet' – this the residual United Irishman who
had been so savagely executed less than thirty years
before! His detractors have tended to see him as
a Whig poodle but he was publicly critical of the
Liberator and might, had he lived in Dublin, have
tended towards Young Ireland. His great positive
act of patriotism was to break down England's
indifference to the distressful country to the west.
He made the English realise that the peasants they
patronised or mocked – when they thought about
them at all – were not the simian clowns of *Punch*
but a people of no mean worth. Moore's contri-
bution to the rebuilding of the Irish nation was
rather more significant that his hoarser critics
allow.

5

'WHEN IN DEATH
I SHALL CALM RECLINE'

After Bannow, there were no more moments of
glory. He continued to make books as Longmans
commissioned them. The *History of Ireland*
spread to four volumes and he found the work,
for which he was temperamentally unsuited,
wearisome. The idea for the book was first
bruited in 1829, when he agreed to do for Erin
what his friend Sir Walter Scott had contracted
to do for Caledonia, stern and wild. Scott
suffered a paralytic stroke after completing two
volumes in 1830 and died two years later;
Moore kept grimly on, finishing with Volume
IV (1846), a total of 1,380 weary pages. Life at
Sloperton was pleasant enough and he had
many visitors and corresponded with a host of
literary and political friends.

The death of his children bore heavily upon him. Barbara, the first-born, died in 1826 of a fall when she was fourteen. Anastasia, the father's favourite, was born in 1813 and survived to be sent to school at Bath. When she was sixteen she became lame in one leg and died in March 1829. Moore sat with her as she struggled with tuberculosis. At one moment towards the end she began to sing her father's favourite of all the *Melodies:* 'When in Death I Shall Calm Recline'. Moore could never face death, and left the room, unable to speak. All the arrangements were left to Bessy, and neither parent attended the funeral, the wife acquiescing in Moore's need to distance himself from mortality. Olivia Byron, who was born in August 1814, died the following March. The first of two sons, Thomas Landsowne Parr, arrived to great rejoicing on 24 October 1818. He assumed himself to be the son of a rich man and regarded the economies practised by his parents as evidence of meanness instead of necessary frugality. His life was straight from Victorian melodrama: the spoilt, handsome son of worthy but indulgent parents. His school career at Marlborough and Charterhouse was undistinguished and, as the holder of an expensively purchased commission in the army, he was eternally in scrapes over drink, women and unpaid debts. He sold his commission and, having joined the French Foreign Legion, died in Algiers in 1845. The baby of the family and Bessy's pet, John Russell, was a much more dutiful son. He had been accepted as a cadet in the army of the East India Company but he too fell a victim to tuberculosis and was sent home from Bengal, to die in 1842, when he was just nineteen.

Moore was spared the prospect of the imminence of his own death. He had a stroke in 1847 and by 1849 was senile, with few intervals of coherence. Bessy tended him with the cheerful care that she had always shown. He died peacefully on 26 February 1852, three months short of his seventy-fifth birthday. His Protestant wife made sure that the Catholic priest who had heard his confession a few years earlier was there to offer him the consolation of the religion he had only intermittently practised. He was buried beside two of his children in Bromham Churchyard, close to the cottage. In his will, he left everything to Bessy, but, of course, there was nothing to leave. Still, she had the pension and she was able to buy an annuity with £3,000 offered by Longmans for the *Journal* – provided Lord John Russell should edit it. Though he was Foreign Secretary and Leader of the Commons at the time, he did not hesitate. It was his final service to a friend. Bessy was able to live on at Sloperton until 8 September 1865, when she joined the rest of her little family in Bromham.

Moore the eternal boy lived too long for his comfort and reputation. Charm and confident anticipation of forgiveness for all imperfections ill become white hairs. It is best to remember him as the pocket-sized toast of the English drawing rooms, where in his own Lilliputian way he was Erin's best ambassador. He loved to be loved and, if that is a fault, it is a venial one. Such friends as Leigh Hunt and Sir Walter Scott have left tributes to a man – or boy – it was hard to dislike. The first recalled that:

His eyes were as dark and as fine as one would like to see under a set of vine leaves; his mouth generous and good-humoured with dimples: and his manner was as bright as his talk, full of the wish to please and be pleased. He sang and played with great taste on the pianoforte, as might be supposed from his musical compositions. His voice, which was a little hoarse in speaking, softened into a breath, like that of the flute when singing.

According to Scott, 'There is a manly frankness with perfect ear and good breeding about him, which is delightful.' John Betjeman, a poet of equivalent popularity, notes in the poem 'Ireland's Own' that:

> In the churchyard of Bromham the yews
>   intertwine
> O'er a smooth granite cross of a Celtic
>   design

and finishes with an appropriate apostrophe:

For the tunes to the elegant measures you
  trod
Have chords of deep longing for Ireland
  and God.

The Minstrel Boy, however, needs no formal tributes. In spite of all his tricks and postures and his unheroic patriotism, he remains for most people, again in Betjeman's words, 'Dear bard of my boyhood, mellifluous Moore'.

A SELECTION OF MOORE'S VERSE

GO WHERE GLORY WAITS THEE

Go where glory waits thee,
But, while fame elates thee,
Oh! still remember me.
When the praise thou meetest
To thine ear is sweetest,
Oh! then remember me.
Other arms may press thee,
Dearer friends caress thee,
All the joys that bless thee
Sweeter far may be;
But when friends are nearest
But when joys are dearest,
Oh! then remember me.

When at eve thou rovest
By the star thou lovest
Oh! then remember me.
Think, when home returning,
Bright we've seen it burning –
Oh! thus remember me.
Oft as summer closes,
When thine eye reposes,

On its lingering roses,
Once so loved by thee –
Think of her who wove them,
Her who made thee love them –
Oh! then remember me.

When, around thee dying,
Autumn leaves are lying,
Oh! then remember me.
And, at night when gazing
On the gay hearth blazing,
Oh! still remember me.
Then, should music, stealing
All the soul of feeling,
To thy heart appealing,
Draw one tear from thee;
Then let memory bring thee
Strains I used to sing thee,
Oh! then remember me.

ERIN, THE TEAR
AND THE SMILE IN THINE EYES

Erin, the tear and the smile in thine eyes
Blend like the rainbow that hangs in the skies;
Shining through sorrow's stream,
Sadd'ning through pleasure's beam,
Thy suns, with doubtful dream,
Weep while they rise!

Erin, thy silent tear never shall cease,
Erin, thy languid smile ne'er shall increase
Till, like the rainbow's light,
Thy various tints unite
And form, in Heaven's sight,
One arch of peace!

'TIS THE LAST ROSE OF SUMMER

'Tis the last rose of summer,
Left blooming alone;
All her lovely companions
Are faded and gone;

No flower of her kindred,
No rosebud is nigh,
To reflect back her blushes
Or give sigh for sigh.

I'll not leave thee, thou lone one,
To pine on the stem;
Since the lovely are sleeping,
Go sleep thou with them;
Thus kindly I scatter
Thy leaves o'er the bed,
Where thy mates of the garden
Lie scentless and dead.

So soon may *I* follow,
When friendships decay,
And from love's shining circle
The gems drop away!
When true hearts lie wither'd
And fond ones are flown,
Oh! who would inhabit
This bleak world alone?

OH, BREATHE NOT HIS NAME

Oh, breathe not his name – let it sleep in the
　　　　shade,
Where cold and unhonoured his relics are laid!
Sad, silent and dark, be the tears that we shed,
As the night-dew that falls on the grass o'er
　　　　his head!

But the night-dew that falls, tho' in silence it
　　　　weeps
Shall brighten with verdure the grave where
　　　　he sleeps
And the tear that we shed, tho' in secret it
　　　　rolls,
Shall long keep his memory green in our souls.

THE MEETING OF THE WATERS

There is not in the wide world a valley so
sweet
As that vale in whose bosom the bright waters
meet.
Oh! the rays of feeling and life must depart
Ere the bloom of that valley shall fade from
my heart!

Yet it was not that Nature had shed o'er the
scene
Her purest of crystal and brightest of green;
'Twas not the soft magic of streamlet or hill;
Oh! no – it was something more exquisite still –

'Twas that friends, the beloved of my bosom,
were near,
Who made every dear scene of enchantment
more dear;
And who felt how the best charms of Nature
improve
When we see them reflected from looks that
we love.

Sweet vale of Avoca! how calm could I rest
In thy bosom of shade, with the friends I love
best,
Where the storms which we feel in this cold
world should cease
And our hearts, like the waters, be mingled in
peace.

THE HARP THAT ONCE
THROUGH TARA'S HALL

The harp that once, thro' Tara's halls,
The soul of Music shed,
Now hangs as mute on Tara's halls
As if that soul were fled –
So sleeps the pride of former days,
So glory's thrill is o'er;
And hearts, that once beat high for praise,
Now feel that pulse no more!

No more to chiefs and ladies bright
The harp of Tara swells;
The chord, alone, that breaks at night,
Its tale of ruin tells: –
Thus Freedom now so seldom wakes,
The only throb she gives,

Is when some heart indignant breaks,
To show that she still lives!

RICH AND RARE
WERE THE GEMS SHE WORE

Rich and rare were the gems she wore,
And a bright gold ring on her wand she bore;
But oh! her beauty was far beyond
Her sparkling gems and snow-white wand.

'Lady! dost thou not fear to stray,
So lone and lovely, thro' this bleak way?
Are Erin's sons good or so cold
As not to be tempted by women or gold?'

'Sir Knight! I feel not the least alarm;
No son of Erin will offer me harm;
For tho' they love woman and golden store,
Sir Knight, they love honour and virtue more!'

On she went and her maiden smile
In safety lighted her round the green isle.
And blest for ever is she who relied
Upon Erin's honour and Erin's pride!

BELIEVE ME, IF ALL THOSE
ENDEARING YOUNG CHARMS

Believe me, if all those endearing young
 charms,
Which I gaze on so fondly today
Were to change by tomorrow, and fleet in my
 arms,
Like fairy gifts fading away,
Thou wouldst still be adored as this moment
 thou art
Let thy loveliness fade as it will;
And around the dear ruin each wish of my
 heart
Would entwine itself verdantly still.

It is not while beauty and youth are thine own
And thy cheeks unprofaned by a tear,
That the fervour and faith of a soul can be
 known,
To which time will but make thee more dear!
Oh! the heart that has truly loved never
 forgets,

But as truly loves on to the close;
As the sunflower turns on her god when he
    sets
The same look which she turn'd when he rose.

LET ERIN REMEMBER
THE DAYS OF OLD

Let Erin remember the days of old,
Ere her faithless sons betray'd her;
When Malachi wore the collar of gold,
Which he won from her proud invader;
When her Kings with standard of green unfurl'd
Led the Red Branch Knights to danger,
Ere the em'rald gem of the western world
Was set in the crown of a stranger.

On Lough Neagh's banks, as the fisherman strays,
When the clear cool eve's declining,
He sees the round towers of other days
In the wave beneath him shining!
Thus shall Memory often in dreams sublime
Catch a glimpse of the days that are over
Thus, sighing, look through the waves of Time
For the long-faded glories they cover.

THE SONG OF FIONNUALA

Silent, O Moyle! be the roar of thy water,
Break not, ye breezes! your chain of repose,
While murmuring mournfully, Lir's lonely
    daughter
Tells to the night-star her tale of woes.
When shall the Swan, her death-note singing,
Sleep with wings in darkness furled?
When will Heav'n, its sweet bell ringing
Call my spirit from this stormy world?

Sadly, O Moyle! to thy winter-wave weeping,
Fate bids me languish long ages away;
Yet still in her darkness doth Erin lie sleeping
Still doth the pure light its dawning delay.
When will the daystar, mildly springing,
Warm our Isle with peace and love?
When will Heav'n, its sweet bell ringing,
Call my spirit to the fields above?
[*Based on the legend of the Children of Lir*]

WHEN IN DEATH
I SHALL CALM RECLINE

When in death I shall calm recline,
O bear my heart to my mistress dear;
Tell her it lived upon smiles and wine
Of the brightest hue, while it lingered here:
Bid her not shed one tear of sorrow
To sully a heart so brilliant and light;
But balmy drops from the red grape borrow,
To bathe the relic from morn to night.

When the light of my song is o'er
Then take my harp to your ancient hall;
Hang it up at that friendly door
Where weary travellers love to call:
Then if some Bard who roams forsaken
Revive its soft note in passing along,
Oh! let one thought of its master waken
Your warmest smile for the child of Song.

Keep this cup, which is now o'erflowing,
To grace your revel when I'm at rest;
Never, oh! never its balm bestowing

On lips that beauty has seldom blest!
But when some warm devoted lover
To her he adores shall bathe his brim,
Oh! then my spirit around shall hover,
And hallow each drop that foams for him.

LOVE'S YOUNG DREAM

Oh! the day's are gone when beauty bright
My heart's chain wove;
When my dream of life from morn till night
Was love, still love!
New hope may bloom
And days may come,
Of milder, calmer beam,
But there's nothing half so sweet in life,
As love's young dream!

Tho' the bard to purer fame may soar
When wild youth's past;
Tho' he win the wise who frowned before
To smile at last;
He'll never meet
A joy so sweet
In all his noon of fame,

As when first he sung to woman's ear
His soul-felt flame,
And at ev'ry close, she blushed to hear
The one loved name!

Oh! that fairy form is ne'er forgot,
Which first love traced;
Still it ling'ring haunts the greenest spot
On mem'ry's waste!
'Twas odour fled
As soon as shed;
'Twas morning's winged dream!
'Twas a light, that ne'er can shine again
On life's dull stream!
Oh! 'twas light, that ne'er can shine again
On life's dull stream!

SHE IS FAR FROM THE LAND

She is far from the land where her young hero
   sleeps,
And lovers around her are sighing;
But coldly she turns from their gaze and
   weeps,
For her heart in his grave is lying!

She sings the wild songs of her dear native
      plains,
Ev'ry note which he loved awaking;
Ah! little they think who delight in her strains,
How the heart of the Minstrel is breaking!

He lived for his love, for his country he died,
They were all that to life had entwined him;
Nor soon shall the tears of his country be
      dried,
Nor long will his love stay behind him.

Oh! make her a grave where the sunbeams rest,
When they promise a glorious morrow;
They'll shine o'er his sleep, like a smile from
      the West,
From her own loved Island of Sorrow!

AT THE MID HOUR OF NIGHT

At the mid hour of night, when stars are
weeping, I fly
To the lone vale we loved, when life shone
warm in thine eye;
And I think that, if spirits can steal from the
region of air
To visit past scenes of delight, thou wilt come
to me there
And tell me our love is remember'd ev'n in
the sky!

Then I sing the wild song which once 'twas
rapture to hear.
When our voices, both mingling, breathed like
one on the ear;
And as Echo far off through the vale my sad
orison rolls,
I think, oh my love! 'tis thy voice from the
kingdom of souls,
Faintly answering still the notes that once
were so dear.

THE YOUNG MAY MOON

The young May moon is beaming, love;
The glow-worm's lamp is gleaming, love;
How sweet to rove
Through Morna's grove,
While the drowsy world is dreaming, love!
Then awake – the heavens look bright, my
dear!
'Tis never too late for delight, my dear!
And the best of all ways
To lengthen our days
Is to steal a few hours from the night, my dear!

Now all the world is sleeping, love,
But the Sage, his star-watch keeping, love,
And I, whose star
More glorious far,
Is the eye from that casement peeping, love!
Then awake – till rise of sun, my dear!
The Sage's glass we'll shun, my dear,
Or, in watching the flight
Of bodies of light
He might happen to take thee for one, my
dear!

THE MINSTREL BOY

The Minstrel Boy to the war is gone,
In the ranks of death you'll find him;
His father's sword he has girded on,
And his wild harp slung behind him.
'Land of song!' said the warrior bard,
'Though all the world betrays thee,
One sword, at least, thy right shall guard,
One faithful harp shall praise thee!'

The minstrel fell but the foeman's chain
Could not bring that proud soul under;
The harp he loved ne'er spoke again,
For he tore its chords asunder;
And said, 'No chain shall sully thee,
Thou soul of love and bravery!
Thy songs were made for the pure and free,
They shall never sound in slavery!'

FAREWELL! BUT WHENEVER YOU WELCOME THE HOUR

Farewell! – but whenever you welcome the
hour,
Which awakens the night-song of mirth in
your bower,
Then think of the friend, who once welcomed
it too,
And forgot his own griefs to be happy with you.
His griefs may return – not a hope may remain
Of the few that have brighten'd his pathway
of pain,
But he ne'er will forget the short vision that
threw
Its enchantment around him, while ling'ring
with you!

And still on that evening, when pleasure fills
up
To the highest top sparkle each heart and each
cup,
Where'er my path lies, be it gloomy or bright,

My soul, happy friends! shall be with you that
     night;
Shall join in your revels, your sports and your
     wiles,
And return to me, beaming all over with
     smiles!
Too blest, if it tells me that, 'mid the gay cheer,
Some kind voice had murmur'd, 'I wish he
     were here!'

Let Fate do her worst, there are relics of Joy,
Bright dreams of the past, which she cannot
     destroy,
Which come in the night-time of sorrow and
     care
And bring back the features that joy used to
     wear.
Long, long be my heart with such memories
     fill'd!
Like the vase, in which roses have once been
     distill'd,
You may break, you may ruin the vase, if you
     will;
But the scent of the roses will hang round it
     still.

HAS SORROW
THY YOUNG DAYS SHADED?

Has sorrow thy young days shaded,
As clouds o'er the morning fleet?
Too fast have those young days faded
That even in sorrow were sweet.
Does Time with his cold wing wither
Each feeling that once was dear?
Come, child of misfortune! come hither,
I'll weep with thee tear for tear.

Has Love to that soul so tender
Been like our Lagenian mine,
Where a sparkle of golden splendour
All over the surface shine?
But if in pursuit we go deeper,
Allured by the gleam that shone,
Ah! False as the dream of the sleeper,
Like Love the bright ore is gone.

Has Hope, like the bird in the story,
That flitted from tree to tree,
With the talisman's glitt'ring glory –

Has Hope been that bird to thee?
On branch after branch alighting,
The gem did she still display,
And, when nearest and most inviting,
Then waft the fair gem away.

If thus the sweet hours have fleeted
When Sorrow herself look'd bright,
If thus the fond hope has cheated,
That led thee along so light;
If thus the unkind world wither
Each feeling that once was dear;
Come, child of misfortune! Come hither,
I'll weep with thee tear for tear.
[*Lagenia: Moore's Latinate version of Leinster*]

THE TIME I'VE LOST IN WOOING

The time I've lost in wooing,
In watching and pursuing
The light that lies
In Woman's eyes,
Has been my hearts undoing.
Tho' Wisdom oft has sought me,

I scorned the lore she brought me;
My only books
Were Woman's looks,
And Folly's all they've taught me.

Her smile when Beauty granted,
I hung with gaze enchanted,
Like him, the Sprite,
Whom maids by night
Oft meet in glen that's haunted.
Like him, too, Beauty won me,
But while her eyes were on me,
If once their ray
Was turn'd away,
O! Winds could not outrun me.

And are these follies going?
And is my proud heart growing
Too cold or wise
For brilliant eyes
Again to set it glowing?
No – alas! th'endeavour
From bonds so sweet to sever –
Poor Wisdom's chance
Against a glance
Is now as weak as ever.

I SAW FROM THE BEACH

I saw from the beach, when the morning was
     shining,
A bark o'er the waters moved gloriously on;
I came when the sun o'er that beach was
     declining;
The bark was still there but the waters were
     gone!

Ah! Such is the fate of our life's early promise,
So passing the springtide of joy we have
     known;
Each wave that we danced on at morning ebbs
     from us,
And leaves us at eve on the bleak shore alone.

Ne'er tell me of glories, serenely adorning
The close of our day, the calm eve of our night,
Give me back, give me back the wild freshness
     of Morning,
Her clouds and her tears are worth evening's
     best light.

Oh! who would not welcome that moment's
returning,
When passion first waked a new life through
his frame,
And his soul, like the wood that grows
precious in burning,
Gave out all his sweets to love's exquisite
flames.

OFT IN THE STILLY NIGHT

Oft in the stilly night,
Ere Slumber's chain has bound me,
Fond memory brings the light
Of other days around me;
The smile, the tears
Of boyhood's years
The words of love then spoken;
The eyes that shone
Now dimmed and gone,
The cheerful hearts now broken!
Thus, in the stilly night,
Ere Slumber's chain has bound me,
Sad Memory brings the light
Of other days around me.

When I remember all
The friends, so link'd together,
I've seen them round me fall,
Like leaves in wintry weather;
I feel like one
Who treads alone
Some banquet-hall deserted,
Whose lights are fled, Whose garland's dead,
And all but he departed!
Thus, in the stilly night,
Ere Slumber's chain has bound me,
Sad Memory brings the light
Of other days around me.

SELECT BIBLIOGRAPHY

Brown, T. 'Thomas Moore: A Reputation' in *Ireland's Literature*. Dublin, 1988.

MacCall, S. *Thomas Moore*. Dublin, 1935.

Moore. T. *The Memoirs, Journal and Correspondence*. (ed. Lord John Russell). London, 1853–6.

Strong, L. A. G. *The Minstrel Boy*. London, 1937.

White, T. de V. *Tom Moore: The Irish Poet*. London, 1977.